The

Cosmic

Unfoldment

Written by:

Robyn Atamian

WestBow
PRESS

WestBow Press books may be ordered through booksellers or by contacting:

WestBow Press
A Division of Thomas Nelson
1663 Liberty Drive
Bloomington, IN 47403
www.westbowpress.com
1-(866) 928-1240

Because of the dynamic nature of the Internet, any Web addresses or links contained in this book may have changed since publication and may no longer be valid. The views expressed in this work are solely those of the author and do not necessarily reflect the views of the publisher, and the publisher hereby disclaims any responsibility for them.

ISBN: 978-1-4497-0212-0 (sc)
ISBN: 978-1-4497-0213-7 (e)

Library of Congress Control Number: 2010926341

Printed in the United States of America

WestBow Press rev. date: 8/2/2010

Dedication

I dedicate this book to my father and mother, Robert and Virginia Atamian.

God has blessed me with one of the world's most wonderful Dads and Moms ever. They have always been there for me whenever I have ever needed them and they have stuck with me through thick and thin. They have also helped guide me through life with their brilliant minds. I would not be alive today if it were not for the unconditional love that I received from my Mom and Dad all throughout my life. It was solely because of their generosity that I was able to write this book. I am so blessed to have parents that care about me. I am very grateful to God. I love them more than anything in the world.

Thank you Mom and Dad

God bless you always.

Forward

I want to send my love to my brothers, Robbie and Terry Atamian. Robbie and Terry are the two most forgiving people that I have ever met. I feel very blessed to have them as my brothers. I love them very much.

And also to the two loves of my life, Sky and Snowflake, my two adorable Chihuahuas. They have brought so much joy into my life. They are truly a gift from God.

I couldn't list everyone so I send my love to all who have touched my life. Thank you.

I want to thank Elaine Doolittle for editing my book. Elaine also helped design the cover of this book.

(If there is ever any glory attached to this book, the glory belongs to God.)

Table of Contents

Appendix

"Self- Reliance"

When I questioned myself in writing this book, it was Ralph Waldo Emerson's essay "Self-Reliance" that gave me the courage to write this book.

Quotes

"As long as I am in the world, I am the light of the world."
John 9: 5

"Know ye not that ye are the temple of God, and that the Spirit of God dwelleth in you?"
1 Corinthians 3: 16

Saul taught: What the prophets and Moses said:
"That the Messiah would suffer and be the first to rise from the dead, and that He would bring Light to the Jews and Gentiles alike."
Acts 26:23

"Where there is no vision, the people perish."
Proverbs 29:18

"Science without religion is lame. Religion without science is blind."
Albert Einstein

Science

God is behind the science.

Electromagnetism

I have found different scientists that have been known to have discovered electromagnetism, Hans Christian Orsted and Michael Faraday among them.   Michael Faraday was a very religious man who became interested in science because he, like Albert Einstein, wanted to use science to discover the hidden mysteries of God.

Electromagnetism is the physics of electricity and magnetism. A physicist discovered that magnetic fields radiate from all sides off of a wire carrying an electric current. Anywhere there is an electric current, there is a magnetic field. They co-exist.

My introduction to electromagnetism came from studying NOVA's films on Albert Einstein.

Electromagnetism was one of the tools that Albert Einstein used to discover his Special Theory of Relativity, $E=mc^2$.

Spiritual Electromagnetism

Spiritual Electromagnetism is what connects the scientific with the spiritual. It is the Light that lives within all of us that is full of God's power.

We all have spiritual energy/electricity within us. This spiritual energy/electricity creates our magnetic fields. They interact just like electromagnetism is the interaction of electric fields and magnetic fields. Therefore, Spiritual Electromagnetism is the physics from the Spiritual Realm brought to life.

Spiritual Electromagnetism is the source of life itself. We are alive because of our Spiritual Electromagnetic energies. We consist of our physical bodies, our Spiritual Electromagnetic energies, and our souls.

The spiritual energy/spiritual electricity (or Spiritual Electromagnetism) current within us, which is light, produces its own magnetic field which surrounds us. The more powerful the current, the more powerful the Light, the more powerful the magnetic field.

There is great creative power in Spiritual Electromagnetism. There is great healing power in it also. It is the spiritual energy source from God. It is the unification of all of life. Spiritual Electromagnetism is the power from God. Spiritual Electromagnetism is the Power of God.

We are most powerful when our Spiritual Electromagnetism or Light is unblocked by negativity and darkness. It is then that the current is open to its fullest capacity. When the Spiritual Electromagnetism or Light can travel freely, we are most powerful.

The way it operates in our lives is for us to be Holy to the best of our ability because Holiness is all pure Light. So if we want to be full of Spiritual Electromagnetism, then we must become Holy.

A Glimpse Into Life

The Universal Law of Equality

God sure wasn't kidding when He told us in the Bible that all men have been created equal. And I say, "and created equal they shall stay,"

Picture a circle and then put a line going across the circle. I call this line the Line of Equality.

Where we fall into danger is when we exalt ourselves above others, and rise above the Line of Equality.

Say we rise 40% above the line of equality. If we rise above others 40% then we will fall beneath others 40% because it will always balance itself out. The same degree that we go up will be the exact same degree that we will fall.

That is why we are meant to treat all people equal to us. The Universal Law of Equality is always operating in all of our lives all of the time.

"And He hath made from one blood every nation of men to dwell on all the face of the earth,"
Acts 17: 26

Holy Spirit

The Holy Spirit is that "still, small voice" we all have within us. The Holy Sprit is our guide and the director of our lives, among many other things.

God gave every single person alive the Holy Spirit. The Holy Spirit dwells within everyone, no matter what religion or creed. The Holy Spirit is one- third of the Godhead.

"While Peter yet spake these words, the Holy Ghost fell on all them which heard the word. And they of the circumcision which believed were astonished, as many as came with Peter, because that on the Gentiles also was poured out the gift of the Holy Ghost".
Acts 10: 44

Some people think that God doesn't have "time" for them. Well that is why God gave "all" of us the Holy Spirit, to help us individually. The Holy Spirit's focus is entirely upon you. We each have the Holy Spirit living within us. The Holy Spirit is waiting to get instructions from you. So Pray, and activate your faith but always pray in the name of Jesus Christ. The Holy Spirit is an intercessor with Jesus Christ and Our Father God Almighty.

Because we all have the Holy Spirit living within us, that means that the spirit of Jesus Christ lives within all of us also. Because they are interwoven, they are both God.

"At that day ye shall know that I am in my Father, and ye in me, and I in you."

John 14: 20

"What? Know ye not that your body is the temple of the Holy Ghost which is in you, which ye have of God, and ye are not your own?
For ye are bought with a price: therefore glorify God in your body, and in your spirit, which are God's."

1 Corinthians 6: 19-20

"Howbeit when He, the Spirit of truth, is come, He will guide you into all truth: for He shall not speak of Himself; but whatsoever He shall hear, that shall He speak: and He will shew you things to come."

John 16: 13

All religions are united by the fact that The Holy Spirit dwells within each and every one of us. No matter what religion, no matter what race you come from, God is dwelling within you in the person of the Holy Spirit.

The Holy Spirit dwells within everyone, everywhere and at all times. And because of this, the Holy Spirit unites the world together.

"The love of God is shed abroad in our hearts by the Holy Ghost which is given unto us."

Romans 5: 5

The Holy Spirit gives us promptings and we are always sorry when we don't obey those promptings. We have to be careful not to let our reasoning mind get in the way of those promptings from the Holy Spirit.

"And grieve not the Holy Spirit of God, whereby ye are sealed unto the day of redemption. Let all bitterness, and wrath, and anger, and clamour, and evil speaking, be put away from you, with all malice: And be ye kind one to another, tenderhearted, forgiving one another, even as God for Christ's sake hath forgiven you."
Ephesians 4: 30-32

Listen to this. One day I was out in my car and that "still, small voice" within me was screaming at me to go to my parents' home, where my sister was staying. But I was mad at my sister for something, so I turned around and went home and took a nap. When I woke up around 5 pm, I got a phone call. My sister was dead. She committed suicide at my parents' home that day. Try to live with that one.

I didn't know then that the voice that was screaming at me was the voice of the Holy Spirit. No one had ever told me that. I wish I had known then that that voice was the voice of the Holy Spirit. I might have been able to save my sister's life. I just never knew that it was the Voice of God.

Well, that's how "serious" it is that we listen and obey and let the Holy Spirit run our lives and keep our own reasoning mind out of the way.

There is so much to be said about The Holy Spirit. Do you know what? It says in the Bible that if you say bad things about Our Father God Almighty and if you say bad things about Jesus Christ, that it will be forgiven of you. But if you say anything bad about The Holy Spirit that it will "not" be forgiven of you. Wow, can you imagine that? What POWER...

Prayer

Prayer is one of the most powerful forces in this world. Prayer has a lot of power in it when we pray the correct way, when we pray with unconditional love, unwavering faith and good will towards all. This is all positive energy. This is all Light.

God may have to put you into the fire for a while, because He might need to mold you into the person you must become. Sometimes you have to be patient and wait on God. Other times your prayers will be answered quickly.

All that you have to do to do your part is to just get ready for it. Work hard at moving right towards your vision. You know what? It will be just around the time that God feels you are ready and a miracle will occur and it will in some way manifest in your life. That is why we must always be working at preparing for it.

Miracles do happen, so get yourself ready for one.

Most importantly it is crucial that when we pray, we send out good will to absolutely everyone. Otherwise it will hinder our prayers from being answered because there can be no darkness in us at all. The more Light that we generate, the more powerful we will become.

It will be God's power working in and through your life. Write out your vision and stay connected to your vision, and do not waver. Only see yourself "connected" to your vision. If you have a dream in your heart then you have vision. Allow your Light (Spiritual Electromagnetism) to come right through you without any obstruction. Get yourself ready and watch your vision come to pass in your life. By being righteous, you will manifest the Divine Plan for your Life.

When I first started writing this book, I made a formula for prayer. When I began to use it, everything started coming to me in fives. But I was more interested in figuring out how it worked, rather than just using it, I have revealed this formula all throughout this book. When you put this to use in your life, and you follow all of my guidelines, watch out because it will change your life. The power really does work.

I'll tell you one thing, that when you do apply this to your life, it will make you happy, really happy. You will be happier than you have ever been in your life, and you will finally have peace.

Emotions

In the Bible, God tells us that there is a season, a time for every purpose under Heaven in which we all experience a variety of emotions, both happy and sad. It is human nature to do so.

The problem arises if we stay stuck in unhappy emotions because they might be debilitating, and we don't want to cling to any emotions that might steal our happiness.

The important thing is that we must look for the positive that comes out of every seemingly negative experience that we have. There is always something positive in all of the pain that we experience.

No matter what comes against us, we should always try to be upbeat. As my sister Ginger always said, "I can't wait to see the good that is going to come out of this for me."
Ginger Atamian

She may have surrendered, but she tried.

Despair

Despair is when you feel that you have lost all hope. This is when it is hard for you to see any light at the end of the tunnel. Everything appears dark.

God promises in the Bible that He will never give us more than we can withstand.

If you are suffering from despair you must begin to change your consciousness immediately. Speak to Jesus even if you have never spoken to Him before in your life. Start now! Start right now!!!

You must take control of your life back. Take back your Power. It is you and God alone that make the decisions that run your life.

You must know that you are in control of your own life. Take hold of the reins.

Is your state of despair caused by some form of depression? Is your depression caused by the fact that you don't really love yourself? Why do you think that you don't love yourself? Have you ever tried to find an honest answer to that question? The answer to that question might help you with your depression.

We "need" more love in the world, and it all begins with "us".

Unconditional Love

Unconditional love is when we can love all people everywhere with no boundaries placed upon our love for them whatsoever. It is when we can love people with no conditions placed upon our love for them.

Unconditional love is when we can love and respect all people everywhere. It is total acceptance of everyone.

It is our ability to love the unlovable.

Unconditional love is very powerful. It has the power within it to break down all barriers. It has the power within it to tear down walls that separate people.

It is total freedom from the darkness because it is all Light. It is pure Light. It is very powerful. It is one of the most powerful forces in the world.

Hate

If you happen to be someone that feels hatred towards anyone you must know that it will hold you back and stunt your spiritual growth. It is a very strong negative emotion to be carrying around. Its energy is pure darkness. It also blocks the channel so that Light can't get through. If you hold onto this hatred, it does have the capacity of hurting you. The only way out of this is to pray for and send good will to anyone that you feel you hate. This is the only way out of this bondage of darkness.

So decide now that you want to improve the quality of your life. You don't want to have any darkness in you at all. All it will do is to hinder good things from coming into your life.

Decide now that it isn't worth it to hold onto any darkness in your life.

Instead, pray yourself out of it. Let go of the hatred. Set yourself free. Let the Light flow through you without any obstruction. This will bring peace into your life and it will improve the quality of your entire life.

"He that saith he is in the light, and hateth his brother, is in darkness even until now. He that loveth his brother abideth in the light, and there is none occasion of stumbling in him. But he that hateth his brother is in darkness, and walketh in darkness, and knoweth not whither he goes, because that darkness hath blinded his eyes."
1 John 2:9-11

Modesty

God calls for each of us to be modest and humble.

In order to do that, we must release our egos and we must be living in a place of pure love. When you are truly modest, you are a loving, kind, sensitive person.

People who are modest would never go around bragging and boasting and being full of pride. They would never want to hurt anyone's feelings or make anyone feel bad because the other person doesn't have something that they may have. They are considerate of others.

Pride

The opposite of modesty is pride. When you are proud you are headed on a downhill spiral. If people don't bring you down, the universe will. There is no escaping the danger of pride. Pride is not Godly and it is not Holy. It is all ego. It is all negative energy and it will throw you into the darkness.

Lucifer tried to rise above God because he was so full of pride, and look at what happened to him. He got thrown right out of Heaven. He was so full of himself. All ego.

Be modest, be a loving person and it will serve you well.

"And whoever exalts himself will be abased, and he who humbles himself will be exalted".
Matthew 23:12

Ego

Jesus repeatedly tells us in the Bible to be modest and humble. We are not meant to be full of pride because that is all our ego. That is when "we" take credit for the good things that we have in our lives.

In order for us to release our ego, we must acknowledge God for all of the good things we have in our lives and we must give God all the glory for it. When we can acknowledge God for this and show God our gratitude, we are releasing ourselves, our ego, from taking credit for it and we are giving God all of the credit. This is how we liberate ourselves from our ego.

Sometimes someone says or does something to hurt you and you find it difficult to forgive them. It is usually related to your "ego". We all get our egos bruised. That's why we must leave our egos at the door if we want to be like Christ. You notice that Jesus had no ego at all.

On the night before Jesus was crucified, Jesus prayed in the Garden of Gethsemane:
"Saying, Father, if thou be willing, remove this cup from me: nevertheless not my will, but thine, be done."
Luke 22: 42

Peace of Mind

I've always said that there is nothing more precious in this world than having true peace of mind.

You can have all of the riches in this world, but if you don't have peace of mind, all of that will be completely empty.

This is especially true of relationships. You have to ask yourself the question, "Does this person bring me peace of mind, or is all that they do to me is upset me?"

Get out of all relationships where someone is trying to bring you down and hold you back. You only want people in your life that you know are supporting you and encouraging you.

Sometimes people are not always so black and white. That is why we must always follow the lead from the Holy Spirit regarding all of our relationships. If God tells you to stay away from someone, then LISTEN... Once I didn't listen and the people that God warned me to avoid, ended up hurting me very badly. And it is extremely important that we obey God "immediately". Partial obedience is considered not to be obedience at all to God.

God's Will vs. Our Will

It has all been left up to us. We get to choose. We can either choose to do God's will with our lives, or we can choose to live our own lives the way we want. That's why God gave us free will. So we could make our own decisions.

If you are interested in manifesting God's Will with your life, you should choose to be as close to Jesus Christ as you can right now in your life.

Because we are only on this planet temporarily, when I leave this temporary housing, I want to spend "eternity" with Jesus Christ. I love Jesus Christ. Jesus is Divine.

You can be sure of one thing, whatever is in God's Will for your life will always be what is truly best for you. When you decide to manifest God's Will with your life, it takes your life to a whole new dimension.

God's Will for all of us is to become a Holy Nation.

"And to make thee high above all nations which he hath made, in praise, and in name, and in honour; and that thou mayest be an holy people unto the LORD thy God, as he hath spoken."
Deuteronomy 26:19

Judging

"Judge not, that ye be not judged. For with what judgment ye judge, ye shall be judged."
Matthew 7:1-2

If you want to be spared from suffering in your life, then never judge anyone but show love and pray for everyone.

The Bible teaches that love is our most important virtue. We should love and accept each individual the way that God created them, and we should restrain our mouth from saying anything bad about anyone. Or else, somehow and in some way, the exact same judgment we place upon others will come knocking at our door. We are held accountable for all of our words and actions.

Light

"While ye have light, believe in the light, that ye may be the children of light."
John 12: 36

"Ye are the light of the world. A city that is set on an hill cannot be hid. Neither do men light a candle, and put it under a bushel, but on a candlestick; and it giveth light unto all that are in the house. Let your light so shine before men, that they may see your good works, and glorify your Father which is in heaven."
Matthew 5: 14-16

I saw a man who told a story on television about being in an airplane crash. Many people died on the plane. When he watched them die, he could see light coming up from their bodies. He said the light had different degrees of brightness.

This was the Spiritual Electromagnetism leaving their bodies when they died because Spiritual Electromagnetism is Light.

The Spiritual Electromagnetism is with you as long as you are alive, because it is the source of life. The Spiritual Electromagnetism, or Light, leaves you when you die.

The brighter the Light when you pass away, the more you are full of Spiritual Electromagnetism.

Holiness

Holiness is where the Light is. Holiness has no negative energy in it at all because it is totally without sin. There is no darkness in holiness whatsoever.

Holiness is all pure Light, and because it is full of Light; it is full of God's divine power.

When we are truly holy we are pure, and because of this we can expect to achieve great things in our lives through prayer. We should all strive to live a holy and peaceful existence.

Jesus Christ was one hundred percent Holy.

Don't you want to be like Jesus?

Holiness is your ticket. Pray to God to cleanse your soul and turn your Light on!

Words

The Bible tells us that we should never use words that would ever slander anyone. And we must never use words that would express a lack of faith in God, such as complaining.

We should only speak uplifting words of faith and belief.

Our words reveal our level of faith and what we truly believe about ourselves (our belief system). Our words also reveal our emotions and what we are feeling. We should be careful to never speak words of doubts, worries and fears, because that is all unbelief. That would only make us frantic, and our goal is to be poised. And when you are poised, you are powerful.

The Bible tells us:
"For by your words you will be justified, and by your words you will be condemned."
Matthew 12:37

God supplies all of my needs.

God's grace blesses my life.

I am full of love.

My love is unconditional.

I am peaceful.

I am merciful.

I am a Light that shines brightly.

I am righteous and holy.

I send good will to absolutely everyone.

I have self-control.

I am in control of my life at all times.

I am loyal and trustworthy.

I am ethical.

I am happy.

I am kind and thoughtful.

I am humble and modest.

I am perfectly healthy and whole.

I am victorious in every area of my life.

I have absolute, unwavering faith.

I am abundant and prosperous.

I am obedient.

I am successful.

I am poised.

I am powerful.

Tongue

"Even so the tongue is a little member and boasts great things. See how great a forest a little fire kindles!

And the tongue is a fire, a world of iniquity. The tongue is so set among our members that it defiles the whole body, and sets on fire the course of nature."

James 3:5

The Bible tells us not to put anyone down, not to speak evil of anyone or judge anyone, not to backbite, defame, slander, whisper gossip, not to have any evil speaking, not to murmur, complain, grumble or gripe. We must never use words that would speak badly of someone because when they find out it will only hurt them. God does not want us to hurt anyone because that is not kind. And God calls for us to be kind. If love is in our hearts, then love will be coming out of our mouths.

The tongue can be very dangerous. We must be careful about every word we speak. We must take this very seriously because the tongue can cause us a lot of trouble.

Tame the tongue.

Forgiveness

The most important thing we need to do in our lives is to forgive everyone we know in our hearts that we need to forgive. When you refuse to forgive someone, you only hurt yourself. You free yourself when you forgive them. In order to truly forgive someone the love has to be stronger than the pain.

Forgiveness is all about love. We should pray for peace in all of our relationships.

As Jesus said from the cross, "Father, forgive them for they know not what they do."
Luke 23:34

Try to remain full of all positive energy and try to love and forgive everyone. Replace hatred with love. When your mind and your emotions are focused on love, then that will bring you into the Light. When you do that, you create all positive energy and it will bring happiness to your life.

When you forgive, you win.

We must have forgiveness with caution.

Our Security is Jesus

What happens when your security leaves you? When the future that you thought you had blows up in your face and disappears? When someone walks out on you, or the person that was taking care of you is no longer able to, or you loose your job. What do you do when your whole world collapses? You must turn to Jesus Christ and become totally dependent upon Him.

You will quickly learn that Jesus is the only real security you have, and you will ever have. Put your faith in God, and trust God for meeting all of your needs. This is what God promises in His Word. God is just changing things around, making adjustments, changing course. Hold on and trust God for His judgment is far superior to ours.

Love

The most important aspect of Christianity is love. God repeatedly tells us the importance of love in the Bible.

Jesus said unto him, Thou shalt love the Lord thy God with all thy heart, and with all thy soul, and with all thy mind. This is the first and great commandment. And the second is like unto it, Thou shalt love thy neighbour as thyself. On these two commandments hang all the law and the prophets.
Matthew 22: 37-40

And the scribe said unto him, Well, Master, thou hast said the truth: for there is one God; and there is none other but he: And to love him with all the heart, and with all the understanding, and with all the soul, and with all the strength, and to love his neighbour as himself, is more than all whole burnt offerings and sacrifices. And when Jesus saw that he answered discreetly, he said unto him, Thou art not far from the kingdom of God. And no man after that durst ask him any question.
Mark 12: 32-34

"A new commandment I give unto you, That ye love one another; as I have loved you, that ye also love one another. By this shall all men know that ye are my disciples, if ye have love one to another."
John 13: 34-35

And to know the love of Christ, which passeth knowledge, that ye might be filled with all the fullness of God.
Ephesians 3: 19

He that hath my commandments, and keepeth them, he it is that loveth me: and he that loveth me shall be loved of my Father, and I will love him, and will manifest myself to him.
John 14: 21

As the Father hath loved me, so have I loved you: continue ye in my love.
John 15: 9

The Father loveth the Son, and hath given all things into his hand.
John 3: 35

But after that the kindness and love of God our Saviour toward man appeared, Not by works of righteousness which we have done, but according to his mercy he saved us, by the washing of regeneration, and renewing of the Holy Ghost; Which he shed on us abundantly through Jesus Christ our Saviour;
Titus 3: 4-6

And hope maketh not ashamed; because the love of God is shed abroad in our hearts by the Holy Ghost which is given unto us.
Romans 5: 5

But God, who is rich in mercy, for his great love wherewith he loved us, Even when we were dead in sins, hath quickened us together with Christ, (by grace ye are saved;)
Ephesians 2: 4-5

Beloved, let us love one another: for love is of God; and every one that loveth is born of God, and knoweth God. He that loveth not knoweth not God; for God is love. In this was manifested the love of God toward us, because that God sent his only begotten Son into the world, that we might live through him. Herein is love, not that we loved God, but that he loved us, and sent his Son to be the propitiation for our sins. Beloved, if God so loved us, we ought also to love one another. No man hath seen God at any time. If we love one another, God dwelleth in us, and his love is perfected in us.
1 John 4: 7-12

And we have known and believed the love that God hath to us. God is love; and he that dwelleth in love dwelleth in God, and God in him.
1 John 4: 16

Love not the world, neither the things that are in the world. If any man love the world, the love of the Father is not in him. For all that is in the world, the lust of the flesh, and the lust of the eyes, and the pride of life, is not of the Father, but is of the world. And the world passeth away, and the lust thereof: but he that doeth the will of God abideth for ever.
1 John 2: 15-17

Herein is our love made perfect, that we may have boldness in the day of judgment: because as he is, so are we in this world. There is no fear in love; but perfect love casteth out fear: because fear hath torment. He that feareth is not made perfect in love. We love him, because he first loved us.
1 John 4: 17-19

"Though I speak with the tongues of men and of angels, but have not love, I have become as sounding brass, or a clanging cymbal. And though I have the gift of prophecy, and understand all mysteries, and all knowledge; and though I have all faith, so that I could remove mountains, and have not love, I am nothing. And though I bestow all my goods to feed the poor, and though I give my body to be burned, but have not love, it profits me nothing. Love suffers long, and is kind; love does not envy; love does not parade itself, is not puffed up, Does not behave rudely, does not seek its own, is not provoked, thinks no evil; does not rejoice in iniquity, but rejoices in the truth; Bears all things, believes all things, hopes all things, endures all things. Love never fails: But whether there are prophecies, they will fail; whether there are tongues, they will cease; whether there is knowledge, it will vanish away. For we know in part, and we prophesy in part. But when that which is perfect has come, then that which is in part will be done away. When I was a child, I spoke as a child, I understood as a child, I thought as a child: but when I became a man, I put away childish things. For now we

see in a mirror, dimly; but then face to face: now I know in part; but then shall I know even as also I am known. And now abide faith, hope, love, these three; but the greatest of these is love."
1 Cor. 13: 1-13

"And above all things have fervent love among yourselves: for love will cover a multitude of sins."
1 Peter 4:8

Behold, what manner of love the Father hath bestowed upon us, that we should be called the sons of God: therefore the world knoweth us not, because it knew him not. Beloved, now are we the sons of God, and it doth not yet appear what we shall be: but we know that, when he shall appear, we shall be like him; for we shall see him as he is. And every man that hath this hope in him purifieth himself, even as he is pure.
1 John 3: 1-3

Greater love hath no man than this, that a man lay down his life for his friends.
John 15: 13

When we pray, it is crucial that we not only have absolute faith, but we need to have unconditional love also. It tells us in the Bible that "faith which worketh by love." (Galatians 5:6)

Our faith will not work if we don't also have love for everyone. In order to be powerful, we cannot have any darkness in us. We must have only Light. That is why "faith worketh by love".

Light and Light together is powerful.

Do not underestimate the power of love.

Do you know what? Love can be fun!

Remember, love never fails.

Obedience

I believe that when God asks for us to be obedient, to quit sinning, that it is more for our good than His. When we sin, it automatically makes us feel disconnected from God because we feel that God might be mad at us. Above all, God desires for all of us to have a close, personal relationship with Him. Sin creates guilt and God does not want us carrying around any guilt. God wants us to be set free of all and any guilt we may be carrying around so that we can feel close to Him again.

Being obedient will make you happy. We must listen to God and obey God. We must know that all He is doing is trying to "protect" us from doing anything that is not good for us. God only wants the best for us. God does not want us to continue in any behavior that He knows could hurt or even destroy our lives. Being obedient to God will protect you from evil. Obedience deadbolts the door to your enemy.

God gave us The Ten Commandments to protect us from evil. God spoke to all of us when He gave Moses The Ten Commandments. They were meant for "all" of God's children. God is still speaking to us today.

Gray Areas

From time to time our lives drift into gray areas and we fall into a rut. There is a way out.

Listen, life is nothing but a series of choices that we make every day. Those choices we make will result in the direction our lives will take. They will ultimately move us toward the Light or the darkness.

See, God is always trying to move us out of our gray areas and move us into the Light. Therefore, we must be full of passion about our lives and our goals and we must dynamically move towards them. We must not be complacent and indecisive because it is this very passion that will take us out of living in the gray areas of our lives and help us to live in the Light.

So go and chase your righteous goals with fierce determination!

Let your Light shine!

Religions

People should be allowed to believe anything that they choose to believe in and still be loved. We should all respect each other's differences and we should strive to be at peace with absolutely everyone.

When we hate people who do not believe in the exact same religion as ours, that is a sin. It is a sin against humanity.

We should all strive to have unconditional love towards everyone no matter what or whom they believe in. This is the starting place, because all of us need to have unconditional love in our lives. It is a very healing force.

We should all strive to live in the Light and we should let that Light transform our world. We should let that Light bring peace to our world.

On Time

Omniscient God already knows every step we will take in life. But because we have free will we can easily change the direction that our lives will go. This will be no surprise to God.

We all have room for improvement in our lives and God can use us at any age.

Sometimes we feel that we should be more advanced than we presently are. We sometimes feel that our mistakes have hindered our progress. But we shouldn't feel that way because in reality this is not true at all. Everything we experience in life is always a lesson, both the good and the bad, and we are growing all of the time. We are exactly where we are meant to be. We are right on time.

Power

Can you imagine pulling bread and fish from the sky to feed the multitudes like what Jesus did? Can you imagine healing the sick? Can you imagine giving sight to the blind, or raising the dead? Can you imagine yourself doing anything like that?

Jesus told us that we would be that powerful.

"Most assuredly I say to you, he who believes in Me, the works that I do, he will do also and greater works than these he will do, because I go to My Father".
John 14:12

Deception

There are some people out there who want to deceive you into believing that they are someone that they aren't (for instance your friend). You must try to see right through these people because they are usually very sneaky. They just may have a hidden agenda.

And what about these people that go around talking "Church, Church, Church", and then they turn out to be really bad people. That is deception.

Deceptive people have the potential of hurting you very badly. They may have no conscience at all for all you know. You should avoid anyone that you feel is deceptive. They could be evil-minded. They could be dangerous. They could possibly be trying to kill you. Just turn on the news and you will see what I mean. Run.

Jealousy

Jealous people can also hurt you very badly. They can be very distressing. All they will do is to try to pull you down. Jealous people find it hard to be a true friend to you because they are not out for your best interests. They are not your friend because they are not "for you". They are incapable of being your friend. They will only wish you ill-will. They are all negative energy. Avoid them at all cost. Think twice before you open up to anyone.

Loneliness

What happens when you feel all alone in the world? Where you feel that all people have deserted you. You feel like no one really cares or loves you at all. What happens when you find yourself all alone like this? When you are really sad.

Just go and write a letter to Jesus, and see if your loneliness doesn't disappear. People wouldn't be so lonely if they had a relationship with Jesus and if they made Jesus their friend. Pour your heart out to Jesus for He is your friend.

Stop being continually hurt by people that have rejected you, and know that Jesus will never reject you.

Just try reaching out to Jesus and make Jesus your friend. You will have a new friend when you do. And you will never have to be lonely again.

Jesus loves you and Jesus wants you to be happy. There is never any happiness or joy when you are deathly lonely.

All that Jesus really wants is for us to love Him, and trust Him. Jesus needs our love just as much as we need His love. And when you do turn to Jesus, Jesus will be waiting.

Prejudice

When you are prejudiced towards someone or some group of people, you are not showing love to them. You are emotionally rejecting them. You may be hurting them by the way you treat them and by the way you might be ignoring them.

The thing that makes you prejudiced towards them could very easily happen directly to you. Instead of being prejudiced towards a particular type of individual, you must have compassion for them instead. Love them the way that God has created them to be. I'll tell you one thing, when we have no compassion for people, God has a way of teaching us to be compassionate.

Overcomers

In life we all have trials and tribulations. We all have to deal with a negative force that exists that is trying to defeat us. We have to guard and protect our lives from this negative force, and we must learn how we can overcome it. It is real and it exists in all of our lives. It will try to destroy our lives if we don't combat it. It is out to take your soul. The negative force is trying to turn you negative. You can't let it. Remember, only the strong survive.

But in order to overcome it, we must train our thoughts to think positive. We must keep our vision, the glorious new future that awaits us, in front of us, and we must stay focused and we must take action. We must emotionally attach ourselves to only what is positive. (Live your life in the Light.) And we must emotionally detach ourselves from everything that is negative. (Stay away from "all" darkness.) Ward off all negative thoughts.

Make yourself dwell upon the positive and see yourself "happy". Win the game that is set before you. Envision yourself happy, really happy, and you have won. You have overcome.

Your "enemy" does not want to see you happy and successful. Your enemy will do everything possible to get you to become down and depressed. And when you become depressed, you self-destruct.

That is why we must stretch our faith and walk by love. We must try our hardest to be happy. Because by being happy you show God that you believe His promises and that you have faith in God. Believing will make you poised. Jesus is always "for you". Jesus wants to see your dreams come to pass. We must live by faith and not by sight, trusting Jesus always.

Remember, your enemy's goal is to try to stop your forward movement.

Witchcraft

It is crucial to your life that you carefully keep all evil spirits out of your life. I am warning you, do not use the Bible like the I Ching. What I mean is, do not ask questions of God and then randomly open up the Bible to try to get your answer. All that is, is witchcraft, and it will not be God answering you, it will be evil spirits. God does not work that way.

Let me tell you a little something about how evil spirits work. They will tell you 20 things that are accurate just to get you to believe the one thing that might destroy your life. Doing this is a very dangerous thing to do. You must keep the door closed against having any evil spirits play with your mind and life. Do not give any evil spirits any power by opening up to them.

Stay clear away from all forms of witchcraft. All forms of witchcraft are evil spirits that you are playing around with.

Hell

Can you imagine being somewhere where you are being constantly tormented and when you shout your prayers out to God to ask for His help, He is not listening? He cannot hear you.

Can you imagine that happening to you?

That is Hell.

Evil begets evil.

Utopia

Can you just envision Utopia? Can you just imagine a life where you have forgiven absolutely everyone? Can you imagine a life where you love everyone unconditionally? Can you just imagine a life where you wish absolutely everyone peace and good will? Can you just imagine a life where you are completely poised and powerful?

This is Utopia.
This is true happiness.
This is peace.

Pearly Gates

Absolutely nothing and no one should ever be able to stop you from boldly walking through those Pearly Gates, and spending eternity with Jesus Christ. Think "eternity".

Mercy

"Blessed are the merciful, for they shall obtain mercy."
Matthew 5:7

God is telling us how deep-rooted our compassion for humanity must be.

Mercy is our ability to love the unlovable, to forgive the unforgivable.

Mercy is God's Grace given to us when we don't deserve it.

God sets no boundaries on His mercy for us, and our mercy for all people everywhere should have no boundaries placed upon it either.

Our mercy should be limitless. Our love should be unconditional.

Healing

When we pray for healing we must keep in mind that sometimes God will heal us instantly in a miraculous way. Sometimes God will heal us through doctors and medicine and sometimes God does not choose to heal us at all.

We must know that God has a purpose in everything that He does. We always have to trust the Lord.

We must all try our best to heal this planet ourselves by becoming as full of positive energy, love, and light as we can be. We all have a part in this drama called Life, and we all have within us the potential to make a real difference in the world.

Unwavering Faith

You have unwavering faith when you pray for something and you begin to trust Jesus Christ immediately. After you have prayed once all you do after that is just thank God and Praise God continuously for the answer to your prayer. By doing this you "show" God that you trust Him. This is how you create unwavering faith. You must have unwavering faith to the point of no doubt.

When we pray we should never take our eyes off of Jesus Christ. We should never take our eyes off of our goal. If we do, and if we start looking around and judging according to appearances, our faith will wither and then our faith will no longer be unwavering.

The apostle Peter's faith was so strong that he walked on water approaching Jesus. When he looked around, he judged according to appearances, and his faith wavered and he began to sink into the water. Unwavering faith is when you keep your faith strong and steady, controlled.

Unwavering faith is very powerful. Faith used correctly is powerful. Combine that unwavering faith with an unconditional love consciousness and that's as powerful as you can get. It is the highest level of achievement. It is a life lived in love.

When you live your life in pure faith, you are poised, and poise equals power. Faith is always calm.

Christianity

Real Christians always point us to Jesus Christ. Jesus Christ is the only true God that has ever lived. Remember, it was Jesus Christ who came to give us our Redemption.

If you are looking for Jesus Christ, just look within yourself, for you will find Him there. Begin to make contact with Him and see how your life changes. You should develop a relationship with Him. All you have to do is just talk to Him like you would a close friend.

Pray to Him and always trust Him. Do not judge according to appearances. Did you know that faith is equated with righteousness? And righteousness with Holiness.

Christianity is something that lives inside of everyone. You can activate it or you can let it lay dormant, but it is there in absolutely everyone. All you have to do is just tap into it to make it real in your life. Jesus Christ is waiting upon you already. He is there for the asking.

In my attempt to try to understand Jesus Christ, I discovered that Christianity was all-inclusive. Because it is pervasive. God exists everywhere in and through every person's life.

I believe in the Trinity, Almighty God (The Father), Jesus Christ (the Son) and the Holy Spirit (the Bearer of Good News). That makes up the Godhead.

They make the rules and the Bible is our Rule Book. Rule number one in my opinion is "obedience". Because from obedience flow all our blessings.

(If you are interested in learning about wisdom, read Proverbs. It is the Book of Wisdom.)

The Rose

If we want to reap a harvest in our lives, then we must first of all, plant the seeds. Then we must nurture the seeds with sunshine and water, and we will watch them grow.

When we first plant the seeds, we have no doubt as to whether they will bear fruit or not. We just automatically believe that they will just as long as we nurture them.

Well if we want to bear fruit in our personal lives, we also need to plant seeds. We must pray, for our prayers are our seeds. Then we must water them with love and give light to them with our faith. We can then bear our fruit.

In nature there is no obstruction to the growth of the flower, the plant, all of nature. They just unfold naturally, with nothing obstructing them. It is a natural Unfoldment.

Well, we should all have our lives unfold just as naturally as the rose. When we can remove all of the darkness and negativity from our lives, we will be removing the obstruction, and our lives will then be able to unfold just as naturally as the rose.

Just keep watering your prayers with your love, and spreading sunshine to them with your faith, and you too will see your dreams unfold just as naturally as the rose.

Imagination

This Earth is like one big movie set. It's like Our Father God Almighty wrote the script, Jesus Christ is the Producer, and the Holy Spirit is the Director. And we are all the actors playing out our own drama.

The good thing is that we can at any time decide to play a different part. We all get to do that. We were given free will and we have the choice to play any part we want.

What part do you see yourself playing? We should play the part that we see in our imagination.

So go ahead and let your imagination liberate you!

Be free!

Fly!

Soar!

William Shakespeare wrote:
    All the world's a stage,
    And all the men and women merely players:
    They have their exits and their entrances;
    And one man in his time plays many parts,
                from As You Like It 2/7

It's All About Love

First of all I am a Christian because I believe that Jesus Christ is God, that He is one-third of the Godhead, but mostly because I love Jesus Christ. In this book I have attempted to awaken you to what I have recently learned about Christianity. This knowledge was revealed to me through the Holy Spirit. And that is my Truth.

I am very aware, however, of the fact that there are people from all over the world that believe in many different theologies. I do not believe that God judges anyone based upon what theology they believe in. Jesus loves the Buddhists just as much as He loves the devoted Christians.

See, I do not believe that it is about theology that counts here on Earth. I believe that it is all about Love. That is what God is looking upon, our hearts, and how much love we spread with our lives. Love supersedes theology. For God loves all of us, no matter what our theology is or is not. Because God is Love.

Appendix

This Little Light of Mine
Written By: Unknown, Copyright: Unknown

This little light of mine,
I'm gonna let it shine
This little light of mine,
I'm gonna let it shine
This little light of mine,
I'm gonna let it shine
Let it shine,
Let it shine,
Let it shine.

Hide it under a bushel? No!
I'm gonna let it shine
Hide it under a bushel? No!
I'm gonna let it shine
Hide it under a bushel? No!
I'm gonna let it shine
Let it shine,
Let it shine,
Let it shine.

This little light of mine,
I'm gonna let it shine
This little light of mine,
I'm gonna let it shine
This little light of mine,
I'm gonna let it shine
Let it shine,
Let it shine,
Let it shine.

Don't let Satan blow it out,
I'm gonna let it shine
Don't let Satan blow it out,
I'm gonna let it shine
Don't let Satan blow it out,
I'm gonna let it shine
Let it shine,
Let it shine,
Let it shine.

This little light of mine,
I'm gonna let it shine
This little light of mine,
I'm gonna let it shine
This little light of mine,
I'm gonna let it shine
Let it shine,
Let it shine,
Let it shine.

Shine all over the world
I'm gonna let it shine
Shine all over the world
I'm gonna let it shine
Shine all over the world
I'm gonna let it shine
Let it shine,
Let it shine,
Let it shine.

This little light of mine,
I'm gonna let it shine
This little light of mine,
I'm gonna let it shine
This little light of mine,
I'm gonna let it shine
Let it shine,
Let it shine,
Let it shine.

Let it shine til Jesus comes,
I'm gonna let it shine
Let it shine til Jesus comes,
I'm gonna let it shine
Let it shine til Jesus comes,
I'm gonna let it shine
Let it shine,
Let it shine,
Let it shine.

This little light of mine,
I'm gonna let it shine
This little light of mine,
I'm gonna let it shine
This little light of mine,
I'm gonna let it shine
Let it shine,
Let it shine,
Let it shine.

Affirmations

I am now a perfect nonresistant instrument for the Will of God to be made manifest in my life.

I will that the Will of God be created in my life.

God's Will, not mine

(Say all the time)

The Ten Commandments

1. I am the Lord thy God and thou shalt not have any strange gods before me.

2. Thou shalt not take the name of the Lord thy God in vain.

3. Remember to keep holy the Lord's Day.

4. Honor thy Father and Mother.

5. Thou shalt not kill.

6. Thou shalt not commit adultery.

7. Thou shalt not steal.

8. Thou shalt not bear false witness against thy neighbor.

9. Thou shalt not covet thy neighbor's wife.

10. Thou shalt not covet thy neighbor's goods.

Jesus taught us to pray the Lord's Prayer.

The Lord's Prayer

Our Father in heaven,

Hallowed be Your Name.

Your kingdom come,

Your will be done

On earth as it is in heaven.

Give us this day our daily bread

And forgive us our debts,

As we forgive our debtors.

And do not lead us into temptation,

But deliver us from evil.

For Yours is the kingdom and the power and the glory forever.

Amen

Twenty-Third Psalm

The Lord is my shepherd, I shall not want. He maketh me to lie down in green pastures. He leadeth me beside the still waters. He restoreth my soul; He leadeth me in the paths of righteousness for His name's sake:

Yea, though I walk through the valley of the shadow of death, I will fear no evil: For thou art with me; thy rod and thy staff they comfort me.

Thou preparest a table before me in the presence of mine enemies; Thou anointest my head with oil; my cup runneth over. Surely, goodness and mercy shall follow me all the days of my life; And I will dwell in the house of the Lord forever.

Daily Prayer

Dear Lord,

Today please bring me help and give me wisdom, guidance, direction, liberty, poise, optimism, perseverance, enlightenment, peace, knowledge, self-control, skill, kindness, compassion, forgiveness, gentleness, happiness, love, fortitude, healing, generosity, meekness, mercy, joy, loyalty, success, fulfillment, diligence, gratitude, devotion, sincerity, patience, stability, clarity, insight, character, confidence, motivation, drive, ambition, belief, determination, unwavering faith, willpower, prosperity, a love for life, cheerfulness, enthusiasm, creativity, respect, authenticity, inspiration, peace of mind, contentment, charm, wit, tenderness, excellence, tolerance, light, honor, good judgment, independence, intelligence, fun, laughter, modesty, discipline, discernment, hope, abundance, power, talent, humility, revelation, honesty, dignity, strength, resilience, integrity, bravery, righteousness, courage, a spirit of holiness, vision, victory, tenacity, grace, safety, protection, perfect health and wholeness, tranquility, an unconditional love consciousness, and illumination.

I believe that I have already received the answer to this prayer in the name of Jesus Christ and I thank you for it now.

Praise the Lord!

I said, PRAISE THE LORD!!!!!!!

Amen

When we are all (righteously) illuminated, we will have Peace on Earth.

Our Position In Christ

We must understand our position of who we are in Christ in order to start living victorious Christian lives. Namely, it is the gift of God's Grace, which was given to all of us from our Lord Jesus Christ before the foundation of the world.

Blessed be the God and Father of our Lord Jesus Christ, who hath blessed us with all spiritual blessings in heavenly places in Christ: According as he hath chosen us in him before the foundation of the world, that we should be holy and without blame before him in love: Having predestinated us unto the adoption of children by Jesus Christ to himself, according to the good pleasure of his will, To the praise of the glory of his grace, wherein he hath made us accepted in the beloved. In whom we have redemption through his blood, the forgiveness of sins, according to the riches of his grace; Wherein he hath abounded toward us in all wisdom and prudence;
Ephesians 1: 3-8

In Christ God has forgiven us all of our sins.
Colossians 2:13

In Christ, we have salvation.
2 Timothy 2:10

In Christ, we will never be separated from the love of God.
Romans 8:39

In Christ, we are sanctified and called to be Holy.
1 Corinthians 1:2

Through Christ and by His name the sick are healed.
Acts 3:16

In Christ, you are called children of God.
1 John 3:1

Through Christ God showed Himself through miracles.
Acts 2:22

In Christ, we receive wisdom, righteousness, holiness, and redemption from God.
1 Corinthians 1:30

Through Christ we are reconciled to God.
2 Corinthians 5:18

"For he hath made him to be sin for us, who knew no sin; that we might be made the righteousness of God in Him."
2 Corinthians 5:21

Through Christ, we are able to speak with authority from God.
2 Corinthians 12:19

In Him and through faith in Him we may approach God with freedom and confidence.
Ephesians 3:12

Scripture

"Then spoke Jesus again unto them, saying, "I am the light of the world: he that followeth Me shall not walk in darkness, but shall have the light of life."
John 8:12

"As long as I am in the world, I am the light of the world."
John 9:5

"I can do all things through Christ which strengtheneth me."
Philippians 4:13

"But my God shall supply all your need according to His riches in glory by Christ Jesus."
Philippians 4:19

"Therefore if any man be In Christ, he is a new creature: old things are passed away; behold, all things are become new."
II Corinthians 5:17

"Nay, in all these things we are more than conquerors through Him that loved us."
Romans 8:37

"Who His own self bare our sins in His own body on the tree, that we, being dead to sins, should live unto righteousness: by whose stripes ye were healed."
1 Peter 2:24

"I am crucified with Christ: nevertheless I live; yet not I, but Christ liveth in me: and the life which I now live in the flesh I live by the faith of the Son of God, who loved me, and gave Himself for me."
Galatians 2:20

"According as He hath chosen us in Him before the foundation of the world, that we should be holy and without blame before Him in love."
Ephesians 1:4

"Blessed be the God and Father of our Lord Jesus Christ, who hath blessed us with all spiritual blessings in heavenly places in Christ."
Ephesians 1:3

"And you, being dead in your sins and the uncircumcision of your flesh, hath He quickened together with Him, having forgiven you all trespasses."
Colossians 2:13

"I thank my God always on your behalf, for the grace of God which is given you by Jesus Christ."
1 Corinthians 1

"For the wages of sin is death; but the gift of God is eternal life through Jesus Christ our Lord."
Romans 6:23

Nor height, nor depth, nor any other creature, shall be able to separate us from the love of God, which is in Christ Jesus our Lord.
Romans 8:39

"And if children, then heirs; heirs of God, and joint-heirs with Christ; if so be that we suffer with Him, that we may be also glorified together."
Romans 8:17

"For He hath made Him to be sin for us, who knew no sin; that we might be made the righteousness of God in Him."
II Corinthians 5:21

"And declared to be the Son of God with power, according to the spirit of holiness, by the resurrection from the dead."
Romans 1:4

Excerpt from "The Circle of Life"
Music by Elton John, Lyrics by Tim Rice

It's the Circle of Life

And it moves us all

Through despair and hope

Through faith and love

Till we find our place

On the path unwinding

In the Circle

The Circle of Life

Epilogue

Ideally we have come to this Earth to manifest God's Will for our lives. We are here to become Holy and Powerful. To become like Jesus Christ. He is our example. When we can turn our righteous and most powerful vision that we hold for our lives into Reality, we will experience The Cosmic Unfoldment.

Allow the Spiritual Electromagnetism within you to light up your life.

Shine as bright as the stars.

And always stay true to your heart.

Peace

Bibliography

PBS NOVA Films
Einstein's Big Idea 2005
Einstein Revealed 1996

http://en.wikipedia.org/wiki/Electromagnetism

http://www.answers.com/topic/electromagnetism

http://www.kididdles.com/lyrics/t030.html

The New Open Bible, New King James Version. Thomas Nelson Publishers, Nashville, 1990.

Bible: King James Version. http://quod.lib.umich.edu/k/kjv/, 1997.

"The Circle of Life"/The Lion King/Walt Disney, Wonderland Music Company. Music by Elton John, Lyrics by Tim Rice, 1994.